My Lord is with Me

The *Du'a'* of Musa (a.s.)

TRANSCRIBED AND ADAPTED FROM
'MY LORD IS WITH ME: THE *DU'AS* OF MUSA (A.S.)' BY
DR. OMAR SULEIMAN

Published by:

Unit No. E-10-5, Jalan SS 15/4G, Subang Square,
47500 Subang Jaya, Selangor, Malaysia
+603-5612-2407 (office) / +6017-399-7411 (mobile)
info@tertib.press
www.tertib.press
@tertibpress (Facebook & Instagram)

Author	:	Dr. Omar Suleiman
Transcriber & Editor	:	Norashikin Azizan
Proofreader	:	Arisha Mohd Affendy
Cover designer	:	Abdul Adzim Md Daim
Typesetter	:	Abdul Adzim Md Daim

MY LORD IS WITH ME: THE *DU'A'* OF MUSA (A.S.)

First Edition: July 2024

Perpustakaan Negara Malaysia

Cataloguing-in-Publication Data

A catalogue record for this book is available from the National Library of Malaysia

ISBN: 978-967-2844-37-2 (hardback)

Copyright © Dr. Omar Suleiman 2024

All rights reserved.
No part of this publication may be reproduced, distributed, or transmitted in any form or by any means, including photocopying, recording, or other electronic or mechanical methods, without the prior written permission of Tertib Publishing.
Printed in Malaysia.

Contents

Foreword	1
Introduction	3
Du'a' in the Qur'an	6
The Essence of Sincere *Du'a'*	9
'Arafah	13
Special *Du'a'* and Prophet Musa (a.s.)	16
Musa (a.s.) and Al-Khiḍr (a.s.)	19
In Trial and Triumph	23
The Story of Musa (a.s.)	27
The Prophets' *Du'a'*	*33*
The *Du'a'* of Musa (a.s.)	42
Glossary	92

Foreword

In the name of Allah, the Most Gracious, the Most Merciful.

It is with great pleasure and reverence that we present *My Lord is with Me: The Du'a' of Musa (a.s.)*, an adaptation of the enlightening lecture delivered by Dr. Omar Suleiman. This book offers a profound exploration of the heartfelt supplications made by one of Allah's most beloved prophets, Musa (a.s.), during his times of trial and triumph.

This adaptation aims to encapsulate the essence of Dr. Omar Suleiman's lecture, translating his spoken words into a written format that retains the depth and warmth of his original message. By delving into the context and significance of Prophet Musa's *du'a'*, we hope to provide readers with a source of spiritual nourishment and a tool for personal reflection and growth.

The story of Prophet Musa (a.s.) is one of resilience, unwavering faith, and the constant presence of Allah's guidance and support. His supplications—uttered in moments of distress and gratitude—remind us of the importance of turning to our Lord in all circumstances. This book not only recounts these pivotal moments but also encourages us to cultivate a similar reliance on Allah in our daily lives.

We are deeply grateful to Dr. Omar Suleiman for his invaluable contributions and for allowing us to adapt his lecture into this written work.

May this adaptation serve as a source of inspiration and a reminder that no matter the challenges we face, *our Lord is always with us.*

With sincere prayers for your benefit,

Tertib Publishing

Introduction

I want to dedicate this beginning to Shaykh Muhammad AlShareef (r.a.h.), *inshā'Allāh*.

When I first received the news of his passing, I considered cancelling my class. Many of you have travelled from different parts of the world to be in the class, and I felt it would be unjust to cancel. Moreover, Shaykh Muhammad AlShareef himself would have encouraged us to continue. He was always about legacy and *ṣadaqah jariyah*, pushing forward even when we felt we couldn't. This class is part of his *ṣadaqah jariyah*, and the entire English-speaking world of *daʿwah* owes a great debt to him, (r.a.h.).

The last time I was in Malaysia, some of you might remember, I wasn't feeling very well. Shaykh Muhammad flew in from Dubai to be with me that weekend. Instead of just hanging out, he became my nurse, buying medicine and checking on me constantly. That's the kind of person he was, (r.a.h.). He made it a point to come, benefit, and spend time with me. While I was teaching, he was right in the front row. When I struggled, he took over a session to give me a break. His generosity and kindness were unparalleled.

Shaykh Muhammad leaves behind a legacy that makes us cry and reflect on the lessons he embodied. *Du'a'* was his favourite subject, and he always emphasised its importance. *How do you make the most of your du'a'? How do you infuse your life with it?* He wanted to hear the story of Ayyub (a.s.) and his *du'a'* because he loved such narratives. As we discuss the *du'a'* of Musa (a.s.), I can't help but think of how much he would have enjoyed this content.

Shaykh Muhammad's father used to take him to *Fajr* every day, shovelling snow to make it easier for others. He taught him the power of *du'a'*, and Shaykh Muhammad carried that passion throughout his life. He wasn't just passionate about his own *du'a'*; he cared deeply about how others made theirs. Whenever someone came to him with a problem, his first question was always about their *du'a'*.

In our personal interactions, Shaykh Muhammad always checked on me, offering beautiful *du'a'* and sincere advice. He reminded me of the importance of *du'a'* and encouraged me to stay positive and productive. He never engaged in drama or negativity. He was always focused on doing good and being productive.

Since this book is about *du'a'*, one thing I find very profound about it is when Allah (s.w.t.) tells us to make *du'a'* for the people that passed away, He says:

$$...رَبَّنَا اغْفِرْ لَنَا وَلِإِخْوَانِنَا الَّذِينَ سَبَقُونَا بِالْإِيمَانِ...$$ (١٠)

Our Lord, forgive us and our brothers who have preceded us in faith.

(al-Ḥashr, 59:10)

One of the ways you can bring *barakah* into your *du'a'* is when you make *du'a'* for those who have passed before you, for those who have gone before you and left behind a beautiful legacy. When you say this *du'a'*, say it with Shaykh Muhammad AlShareef in your heart. Include him in your *du'a'*.

May Allah (s.w.t.) bless him, accept from him, have mercy on him, elevate him, and allow his efforts to continue until the Day of Judgement, with the best of intentions, with *ikhlas*, with *istiqamah*, and allow us to benefit from him and to follow in his footsteps. *Āmīn*.

Imam Omar Suleiman

Du'a' in the Qur'an

The most recorded *du'a'* in the Qur'an are from Prophets Musa (a.s.) and Ibrahim (a.s.). One scholar mentioned that out of all the *du'a'* made from Adam (a.s.) until the Day of Judgement, Allah (s.w.t.) chose only seventy or so to be in His book, the Qur'an. These *du'a'* are special and full of blessings. Consider the last two *ayat* of *surah* al-Baqarah or the *du'a'* that start with '*Rabbanā*.' Of course, the *du'a'* attributed to a prophet are particularly significant.

Allah (s.w.t.) records the *du'a'* of a prophet in private moments. Imagine Zakariyya (a.s.) in the corner of Masjid al-Aqsa, calling upon his Lord. Allah (s.w.t.) records it. The words of Maryam (a.s.) under a palm tree, all by herself; Allah records it for us. The *du'a'* of Ibrahim (a.s.) at every stage of his life, Allah (s.w.t.) records these *du'a'*. And the *du'a'* of Musa (a.s.), throughout the different phases of his life, Allah (s.w.t.) records them.

There is an amazing blessing in these *du'a'*, and of course, in all the *du'a'* we learn from the Prophet (s.a.w.). What are we to do with Qur'anic *du'a'* and the *du'a'* from the sunnah? We are to learn from their sequence and build upon them. One problem with *du'a'* is that it can become scripted, as if you are merely reading something. This can defeat the purpose of having an intimate conversation with Allah (s.w.t.) when you are constantly reading from a text or scrolling through screens to find the next word.

Du'a' is supposed to be intimate and personal. You should be able to take the blessings of these *du'a'* and then engage in your own personal conversation with Allah (s.w.t.). Allah (s.w.t.) does not need you to rhyme, be poetic, or even make *du'a'* in Arabic. Your own language, from the heart, following the sequence we learn from the Prophet (s.a.w.) and these blessed examples, is sufficient.

There is an equation; something about each of these *du'a'* that you can take and use to launch into your own personal way of calling upon Allah (s.w.t.). This is especially interesting because Musa (a.s.) himself sought special *du'a'* from Allah (s.w.t.).

The Essence of Sincere *Du'a*

My Lord is with Me

There's something that happens to me quite often, and I believe it happens to many *imam*. Someone will approach and say:

> *"Shaykh, I need a du'a' for my kids."*

So I respond with:

> *"Rabbanā ḥablanā min azwājinā…"*
> *"No, Shaykh, I found this du'a' on WhatsApp. It's like 20 lines long. I don't know where it's from, but is it a good du'a'?"*

So I said:

> *"I just gave you a du'a'."*

Make *du'a'* for your kids in a sincere way. People often seek long, poetic *du'a'* that sound pleasing to the ears. But what Allah (s.w.t.) wants to hear from you is sincere *du'a'*.

Think for a moment. Taif was the hardest moment for Rasulullah (s.a.w.). What if I told you there is not one certain authentic *du'a'* from Taif that is narrated?

Can you believe that? Wouldn't you want to know what Rasulullah (s.a.w.) was saying in Taif? We have a famous *du'a'* that we share, and we take the blessing from it, but it's not authentically narrated like a hadith. We don't derive *fiqh* or *'aqidah* from it or anything like that. We take it because it is beautiful and a blessing.

اللهـم أشكو إليـك ضعـف قوتي، وقلة
حيلتي، وهواني على النـاس

O' Allah, I complain to You of my weakness, my scarcity of resources, and the humiliation I face from people.

But it is not authentic. It is OK to use and to take blessing from it, but we do not have a single textual reference that the Prophet (s.a.w.) recited this specific *du'a'*. Do you know how significant that is? Because I would want to know what the Prophet (s.a.w.) was saying, right? But he was calling upon Allah in a way that was beautiful and befitting.

Sayyidina 'Ali (r.a.) said that the Prophet (s.a.w.) spent the entire night in the tent with his hands raised, making *du'a'*. When people went to sleep, the Prophet (s.a.w.) spent the whole night making *du'a'*. Yet, we don't have the exact narrations of his words.

ʿArafah

My Lord is with Me

One of my favourite narrations involves the Prophet (s.a.w.) during 'Arafah, where his hands were raised in supplication for such an extended period that his armpits were visible. This narration highlights the Prophet's (s.a.w.) deep love for calling upon Allah.

The companions were uncertain whether to fast on the day of 'Arafah during *hajj*. For seven years in Madinah, they had fasted on this day, but during *hajj*, they were unsure. They were hesitant to interrupt the Prophet (s.a.w.), who was deeply engrossed in his *du'a'*. Various narrations describe what happened next. According to some, Lubabah (r.a.) noticed the Prophet (s.a.w.) and offered him a glass of milk. Understanding their dilemma, the Prophet (s.a.w.) took the glass of milk, held it up, and drank. This action signalled to everyone that they could break their fast. With relief, everyone began to eat, drink, and hydrate themselves in 'Arafah.

Interestingly, we also do not have a specific *du'a'* from 'Arafah, except for the phrase:

لَا إِلَهَ إِلَّا اللَّهُ وَحْدَهُ لَا شَرِيكَ لَهُ لَهُ الْمُلْكُ وَلَهُ الْحَمْدُ وَهُوَ عَلَى كُلِّ شَيْءٍ قَدِيرٌ

There is no deity except Allah, alone, without any partners. His is the dominion, and His is the praise, and He has power over all things.

(Mishkat al-Masabih 1213)

This narration serves as an epitome that *du'a'* is an intimate conversation between you and Allah.

Special *Du'a'* and Prophet Musa (a.s.)

Now we are going to explore the story of Musa (a.s.), which is particularly interesting. This is an authentic hadith recorded in Mishkat al-Masabih 2309. The Prophet (s.a.w.) says: Musa (a.s.) said:

يَا رَبِّ عَلِّمْنِي شَيْئًا أَذْكُرُكَ بِهِ وَأَدْعُوكَ بِهِ

O' my Lord, teach me something that I can call upon You with and I can remember You with.

What do you understand from this? Musa (a.s.) was saying, "Give me a really special *du'a'*, O' Allah."

Musa (a.s.) is *KalīmAllāh*, he speaks directly to Allah and Allah speaks directly to him. Musa (a.s.) asked, "O' Allah, give me a nice *du'a'*. Something private, secret between You and I, that I can call upon You."

The Prophet (s.a.w.) said, Allah responded, "O' Musa, say *lā Ilāha illAllāh*."

Musa (a.s.) said, "Everyone says *lā Ilāha illAllāh*. All of your servants say *lā Ilāha illAllāh*, this isn't what I'm asking. I'm asking you Allah for a really special *du'a'*. Something long, elaborate. Precious between you and me."

And Allah just told Musa (a.s.) the most basic *dhikr*. *Lā ilāha illAllāh*.

Allah responded, "O' Musa, if you took *lā Ilāha illAllāh* and you put it on a scale, and on the opposite of the scale, you put the heavens and the earth and everything in them, *Lā Ilāha illAllāh* will outweigh them all. *Lā Ilāha illAllāh* is a special *du'a'*. Keep on repeating it."

The Prophet (s.a.w.) said the best *dhikr* is *lā Ilāha illAllāh* and the best *du'a'* is *alhamdulillāh*. Follow the mechanism, use them to go to the next level of your *du'a'*. But there is nothing more blessed than *lā Ilāha illAllāh*.

Allah (s.w.t.) does not hide beneficial knowledge like this from us. Someone says, "I'm going to find a *Shaykh* that's going to give me the special *du'a* that will solve all of my problems." But there is nothing more beautiful than the *du'a'* that Allah gave you, the *dhikr* that Allah gave you on the tongue of your Prophet (s.a.w). *Lā Ilāha illAllāh*.

Nothing more blessed than the simple *du'a'* as of the Qur'an and the sunnah of the Prophet (s.a.w). Even Musa (a.s.) sought a special *du'a'* from Allah and was told to say *lā Ilāha illAllāh*. So keep saying it, and just like Musa (a.s.), you will see something very special from Allah.

Musa (a.s.) and Al-Khiḍr (a.s.)

My Lord is with Me

Musa (a.s.) and his *du'a'* are very significant if we understand the constant twists and turns in his life. Recorded in the Qur'an, his story begins as a baby casted into the Nile River to survive a tyrant and ends with him dying near Mount Nebo because his people were disobedient. From the Nile River to Mount Nebo, Musa (a.s.) was always in danger, which led him to continuously turn to Allah.

Some scholars say Musa (a.s.) never had a stable figure in his life. He did not have a spouse who was with him all the time, nor did he have his mother or 'Asiyah (a.s.) consistently by his side. Musa (a.s.) never had someone he could depend on all the time. This is beautifully illustrated in *surah* al-Qaṣaṣ, revealed after the deaths of Abu Ṭalib and Khadijah (r.a.). Like the Prophet (s.a.w.), who could no longer look to Abu Ṭalib for physical protection or Khadijah (r.a.) for comfort, Musa (a.s.) always turned to Allah (s.w.t.) every time he is in need. His *du'a'* reflect *tawakkul* in Allah (s.w.t.).

For better illumination, we are to explore the story of Musa (a.s.) and Al-Khiḍr (a.s.), where Allah sent Musa to Al-Khiḍr to learn about His decree. Although Musa (a.s.) is greater than Al-Khiḍr, he was sent to learn some knowledge he did not yet comprehend. Each incident with Al-Khiḍr relates to Musa's (a.s.) life in some way.

Firstly, people were saved by a destructive act when Al-Khiḍr drilled holes into their ship. Musa (a.s.) could relate to this, as he was saved as a baby placed in a basket and set adrift in the Nile River. The way the ship was saved from pirates by seemingly being destroyed is the same as Musa's mother's act of casting into the river as a baby—to save him from Fir'awn.

The second incident involves an innocent child being killed by Al-Khiḍr without actual reason, reflects the act of Fir'awn killing children of Bani Isra'il. Just like the innocent kid killed by Al-Khiḍr who would grow up to be a disbeliever and oppress his parents to be disbelievers as well, some scholars suggest that the children of Bani Isra'il might have grown up to be among those who would later disobey Musa (a.s.).

Lastly, Al-Khiḍr was building a wall for a group of ungrateful people. This is somehow a foretelling of Musa's (a.s.) own experience with his people during the exodus and exile for forty years. Despite the disobedience of many, Allah (s.w.t.) blessed the next generation because of the righteousness of a few. Al-Khiḍr built the wall because of a righteous father whose *du'a'* benefited future generations, illustrating how **outcomes don't always match requests**, but they are always better for you.

The story of Musa (a.s.) and Al-Khiḍr is a reflection of how paramount *tawakkul* or reliance in Allah (s.w.t.) is. Allah's plans are always the better one for us, even when sometimes they seem incomprehensible to us. Again, outcomes as well as divine wisdom don't always match requests and human expectations.

In Trial and Triumph

My Lord is with Me

The Prophet (s.a.w.) connected us to Musa (a.s.) in both trial and triumph. In times of hardship, even the Prophet (s.a.w.) would recall Musa's (a.s.) patience. When the Prophet (s.a.w.) was hurt or faced difficulties from his people, he would say, "*Raḥim Allāhu akhī Musa*," meaning, "May Allah have mercy on my brother Musa." This is because Musa (a.s.) was tested with something harder than this, and he was patient.

When you are going through a hard time or someone is giving you a hard time, remember the hardship that Musa's (a.s.) people caused him. Sometimes you might think, "Well, I did good for this person, and they betrayed me or wronged me." But did you save an entire people from a pharaoh, split the sea for them, and lead them to safety? And look at how Musa's (a.s.) people treated him. So when you say, "I did so much good for this person, and this is how they repaid me, and I'm hurting," remember Musa (a.s.). He was deeply hurt but remained patient with Allah's decree.

We also see triumph in the story of Musa (a.s.). We will all be fasting on *'Ashura'* to honour this day. When the Prophet (s.a.w.) arrived in Madinah and saw the Jewish tribes fasting, he asked, "Why are they fasting?" They replied that it was the day Allah gave Musa (a.s.) victory against The Pharaoh. The Prophet (s.a.w.) said, "Then we will take it as a day of fasting." He declared, "We are closer to Musa (a.s.) than you; we are closer to Musa than anyone else." (Ṣaḥīḥ al-Bukhari 2004, Ṣaḥīḥ Muslim 1130) We love Musa (a.s.), and we are connected to him in both hardship and triumph.

There is a reason why the Qur'an mentions Musa (a.s.) more than any other prophet. To be the most talked-about man in the greatest revelation is significant. The Qur'an's frequent references to Musa (a.s.) are meant to connect us to him and his experiences.

Scholars mention that Musa (a.s.) was *KalīmAllāh*, the one to whom Allah spoke directly. Allah says in *surah* al-Baqarah, 2:186:

وَإِذَا سَأَلَكَ عِبَادِى عَنِّى فَإِنِّى قَرِيبٌ ۖ أُجِيبُ دَعْوَةَ ٱلدَّاعِ إِذَا دَعَانِ ۖ فَلْيَسْتَجِيبُوا۟ لِى وَلْيُؤْمِنُوا۟ بِى لَعَلَّهُمْ يَرْشُدُونَ ﴿١٨٦﴾

> And when My servants ask you, [O Muḥammad], concerning Me—indeed I am near. I respond to the invocation of the supplicant when he calls upon Me. So let them respond to Me [by obedience] and believe in Me that they may be [rightly] guided.

Musa (a.s.) had the unique privilege of speaking to Allah directly on Earth, without an angel as an intermediary. This unique place with Allah (s.w.t.) highlights the special nature of his dialogue with Allah.

The Story of Musa (a.s.)

My Lord is with Me

It starts off with Musa (a.s.) growing up in the palace of Firʿawn. Interestingly, Musa (a.s.) had a relatively uneventful life from the time he was put into the river and found, until this point in his adult life. There were not too many twists and turns.

Have you ever noticed that when the tests of Allah come, when it rains, it pours? Things might be going very smoothly, and then all of a sudden, it's test after test. That is often how people are tested. Musa (a.s.) grew up in Firʿawn's palace and was clearly privileged. He did not have to go far to see people from his descent, Bani Israʾil, who were slaves. Because of what happened—ʿAsiyah taking him as a son—he grew up in Firʿawn's palace, completely privileged. Although he would never truly be Egyptian or belong to the royalty, he was protected, privileged, and grew up very comfortably.

Nothing significant happens in his early life. We don't see any health challenges, wealth challenges, or any major disturbances. His life was very quiet and uneventful, which sometimes makes the subsequent trials harder to bear because everything was going well, and then everything started going downhill.

One day, Musa (a.s.) went into the city unnoticed

by his people at an odd time. The scholars say that the palaces were on the outskirts of the city. Away from the vicinity of the palace, Musa (a.s.) was walking through the streets of the city, unnoticed by the people. He saw two men fighting, which was not uncommon. Imagine an alleyway or a somewhat isolated place at night; two people were fighting, and Musa (a.s.) observed the situation. Of course, in such situations, you are going to make snap judgements. What do most people do today when they see something terrible happening in front of them? They will stand there and watch. Even worse, fighting to get the best angle to record on their phone camera. How many terrible things happen now, and people just watch? It is an indictment of our *fitrah*. This is not who we are supposed to be. The Prophet (s.a.w.) mentioned that one of the signs of the end times is that people would commit adultery in the middle of the street, and the most righteous person would simply say, "Would you mind, you know, maybe moving to the side?" The idea of intervening against wrongdoing is disappearing.

But Musa (a.s.) was better than that. He was from the palace; he could have said, "OK, I'm going back to the palace. I'll leave these crazy people alone." But he did not. One of the men was from Bani Isra'il, the slave class, and the other was from the ruling class. The exploitation of Bani Isra'il by the Egyptians was commonplace. It was a safe assumption that the Egyptian man was oppressing the man from Bani Isra'il because that was how the society worked.

The man from Bani Isra'il called out to Musa (a.s.) and asked for help. Musa (a.s.) was a strong man; growing up in the palace did not make him soft. This was the man who punches the Angel of Death when the Angel of Death comes to him. Musa (a.s.) intervened and hit the Egyptian man, accidentally killing him. He did not mean to kill him; he just wanted to get him off the man from Bani Isra'il. Musa (a.s.) was so strong that when he struck the Egyptian man, he accidentally killed him. Some scholars say it was a closed-fist punch to the face that killed him.

Musa (a.s.) says, "This is from the work of the devil—he is a clear enemy—he leads people astray." *SubḥānAllāh*, here you have a situation where Musa (a.s.) has a dead man from the ruling class in front of him, and the man from Bani Isra'il has fled the scene. Musa (a.s.) knew that in this moment of trying to do something noble, he was going to end up in a completely devastating situation. He blamed *shayṭan* for the deception but did not escape accountability for himself. He sought Allah's forgiveness, acknowledging his mistake.

Musa (a.s.) knew that despite his privilege, killing someone from the Egyptian ruling class reduces him to just being one of Bani Isra'il. This is the lesson about how racism and tribalism work—you are always disposable.

Now, a few questions to clarify:

Aren't the prophets *ma'sum* or infallible? Yes, prophets are infallible. They do not commit major sins. Then why doesn't Musa's (a.s.) action qualify as a major sin, and why does it not affect his infallibility?

Firstly, Musa (a.s.) was in the right since he intervened at the right time. The man from Bani Isra'il was actually oppressed by the Egyptian man. Therefore, Musa (a.s.) did not misunderstand what was happening.

Secondly, it was not his intention to kill the Egyptian man. He was just trying to stop the oppression. It was not like Musa (a.s.) plotted the murder.

The only mistake Musa (a.s.) made was using too much force. In the heat of the moment, it was an unintended consequence.

Some scholars say this incident happened before Musa (a.s.) was bestowed with prophethood, making it irrelevant in terms of his prophetic infallibility. This is a problem when we read too much of the biblical narrative and import it into Islam. The biblical version paints Musa (a.s.) as executing the Egyptian and then covering it up. But according to the Islamic narrative, Musa (a.s.) was simply a bit aggressive in trying to stop oppression.

Think about how quickly one's situation can change. Musa (a.s.) went from being a privileged individual under Fir'awn's protection to being in a potentially life-threatening situation. This is how *qadar* works—one moment, you are powerful; the next, you are impoverished. Blessings can be taken away very quickly.

The Prophets' *Du'a'*

> "O' my Lord, I wronged myself."

Now you know what the first concern of Musa (a.s.) was?

$$\text{قَالَ رَبِّ إِنِّى ظَلَمْتُ نَفْسِى فَاغْفِرْ لِى فَغَفَرَ لَهُۥٓ ۚ إِنَّهُۥ هُوَ ٱلْغَفُورُ ٱلرَّحِيمُ ﴿١٦﴾}$$

He said, "My Lord, indeed I have wronged myself, so forgive me," and He forgave him. Indeed, He is the Forgiving, the Merciful.

(al-Qaṣaṣ, 28:16)

Remember that he said that *shayṭan* was the one who designed this plan, this plot, but regarding accountability—he does not blame *shayṭan*. You cannot blame *shayṭan* when you make a mistake. You have to take ownership of it. You have to own up right away and be self accountable.

He admitted, "O' my Lord, I wronged myself . So forgive me."

And so Allah forgave him. Allah is Most Forgiving, Most Merciful. It is really profound that the first concern of Musa was not the fact that he will be killed. He was so concerned that Allah would punish him. Oftentimes when we make a mistake then we face worldly consequences—shame, humiliation, punishment—something harmful, So what we are really afraid of is the worldly consequence. Not the consequence from Allah (s.w.t.). Different from Musa (a.s.), he was not worried about Fir'awn killing him as much as he was worried about Allah forgiving him.

If you look at the *ayah*, the letter 'ف' in فَغَفَرَ لَهُ is a result that he asked Allah for forgiveness and Allah forgave him right away.

Allah did not leave him hanging. His *du'a'* was accepted right away. The moment he said, "My Lord, forgive me." Allah (s.w.t.) accepted his *du'a'*.

Allah (s.w.t.) is *al-Ghafūr* and *ar-Raḥīm*; He is the Most Forgiving and the Most Merciful. That is why He forgave Musa (a.s.).

What does that mean for you when you call upon Allah after a sin?

❖ قُلْ يَـٰعِبَادِىَ ٱلَّذِينَ أَسْرَفُوا۟ عَلَىٰٓ أَنفُسِهِمْ لَا تَقْنَطُوا۟ مِن رَّحْمَةِ ٱللَّهِ

$$\text{قُلْ إِنَّ ٱللَّهَ يَغْفِرُ ٱلذُّنُوبَ جَمِيعًا ۚ إِنَّهُۥ هُوَ ٱلْغَفُورُ ٱلرَّحِيمُ ﴿٥٣﴾}$$

Say, "O' My servants who have transgressed against themselves [by sinning], do not despair of the mercy of Allah. Indeed, Allah forgives all sins. Indeed, it is He who is the Forgiving, the Merciful."

(az-Zumar, 39:53)

One might say that they are not Musa (a.s.) who has a special connection with Allah; that they can seek forgiveness from Allah and Allah will forgive them. It is not about who you are, or who Musa (a.s.) is. *It is about who Allah is.*

> "Indeed, I have been of the wrongdoers."

The scholars also say this is similar to the *du'a'* of Yunus (a.s.).

وَذَا ٱلنُّونِ إِذ ذَّهَبَ مُغَٰضِبًا فَظَنَّ أَن لَّن نَّقْدِرَ عَلَيْهِ فَنَادَىٰ فِى ٱلظُّلُمَٰتِ أَن لَّآ إِلَٰهَ إِلَّآ أَنتَ سُبْحَٰنَكَ إِنِّى كُنتُ مِنَ ٱلظَّٰلِمِينَ ۝٨٧

And [mention] the man of the fish [i.e., Jonah], when he went off in anger and thought that We would not decree [anything] upon him. And he called out within the darknesses, "There is no deity except You; exalted are You. Indeed, I have been of the wrongdoers."

(al-Anbiya', 21:87)

It is about being accountable. In this *du'a',* Yunus (a.s.) is admitting that there is no God but Allah and how perfect is Him. He admitted that he was from the wrongdoers and he would not blame his people and their arrogance and stubbornness.

"Our Lord, we have wronged ourselves"

Then we have Adam (a.s.) and Hawwa' (a.s.).

$$\قَالَا رَبَّنَا ظَلَمْنَآ أَنفُسَنَا وَإِن لَّمْ تَغْفِرْ لَنَا وَتَرْحَمْنَا لَنَكُونَنَّ مِنَ ٱلْخَٰسِرِينَ ۝$$

They said, "Our Lord, we have wronged ourselves, and if You do not forgive us and have mercy upon us, we will surely be among the losers."

(al-A'raf, 7:23)

So it is about accountability. When you make a mistake, do not blame *shaytan*, circumstance, or people and just own it. Why is it that when we do something wrong with our parents or with someone else, we don't own it? This is because we are afraid of what they are going to do to us if we own it. That is why we are pointing the blame to someone else. But right now, you are dealing with *al-Ghafūrur-Rahīm*. You are dealing with Allah (s.w.t.) which makes it absolutely different. He (s.w.t.) appreciates it when you own your mistakes.

With Allah (s.w.t.) you do not have to worry or be fearful of ownership in the least. This is because ownership translates to His forgiveness, and that is why in Adam, Yunus and Musa's situation, Allah mentions *fastafahu*. Allah chose them after their mistake. The elevation, the prophethood, the chosenness comes after all three of them make the mistake. Because when you make the mistake and then you own it and seek forgiveness from Allah (s.w.t.), you elevate yourself to a position that was higher than before you made the mistake in the first place.

It is a concept that is foreign to human beings. If you do something bad to someone, then you seek forgiveness; even if they forgave you, they are still going to be suspicious of you. Their trust in you is reduced. The moment you start to show a sign that you are doing it again, then they will compound the consequences on you. This is different with Allah (s.w.t.). After you seek forgiveness, you are in a better situation than before you committed the sin. Sometimes you have to repeat that to yourself a few times and remind yourself. *Tawbah* does not cleanse; it elevates. Looking back at the cases of all three prophets, you have elevation after the mistake—prophethood and chosenness. Adam (a.s.), Yunus (a.s.) and Musa (a.s.) were all better off after the mistake.

So in your *du'a'*, describe yourself as the one who committed the wrongdoing. The version of that in terms of the sin of describing your situation is that I sinned. The version of that in other situations is perhaps I am sick, I am poor, I am broken, I am hurt. So it is important that we describe ourselves as the one who has sinned.

In repentance, there are two things that have to be present. One, acknowledge your sinfulness and two, acknowledge the mercy of Allah (s.w.t.).

The *Du'a'* of Musa (a.s.)

There is a Hadith Qudsi:

> I heard the Messenger of Allah (s.a.w.) say: Allah the Almighty said: O' son of Adam, so long as you call upon Me and ask of Me, I shall forgive you for what you have done, and I shall not mind. O' son of Adam, were your sins to reach the clouds of the sky and were you then to ask forgiveness of Me, I would forgive you. O' son of Adam, were you to come to Me with sins nearly as great as the earth and were you then to face Me, ascribing no partner to Me, I would bring you forgiveness nearly as great as it.
>
> (Hadith 34, 40 Hadith Qudsi)

Allah (s.w.t.) is saying that He forgives you and He does not mind. So your sin has not stained your record.

$$قَالَ رَبِّ إِنِّى ظَلَمْتُ نَفْسِى فَاغْفِرْ لِى فَغَفَرَ لَهُ ۚ إِنَّهُ هُوَ ٱلْغَفُورُ ٱلرَّحِيمُ ﴿١٦﴾$$

He said, "My Lord, indeed I have wronged myself, so forgive me," and He forgave him. Indeed, He is the Forgiving, the Merciful.

(al-Qaṣaṣ, 28:16)

This is the first *du'a'* of Musa (a.s.) that is recorded in the Qur'an from his life; it is a *du'a'* for forgiveness. Actually, this is the case for all prophets. For example, Sulayman (a.s.), when he asked Allah (s.w.t.) for a kingdom, he said, "*Rabbī firghlī...*" which means, "*O' my Lord, forgive me...*"

Therefore, ask Allah for His forgiveness, no matter what else you are asking Him for. This is also a lesson in your *du'a'* as well. Whatever your request to Allah (s.w.t.)—a house, a job, a spouse—start it off seeking Allah's forgiveness. Let that always be the beginning of your *du'a'*.

$$\text{قَالَ رَبِّ بِمَآ أَنْعَمْتَ عَلَىَّ فَلَنْ أَكُونَ ظَهِيرًا لِّلْمُجْرِمِينَ ﴿١٧﴾}$$

He said, "My Lord, for the favour You bestowed upon me, I will never be an assistant to the criminals."

(al-Qaṣaṣ, 28:18)

In this verse, Musa (a.s.) pledged that he would never be the tool for the oppressors as Allah (s.w.t.) has bestowed him with favours—ease, power and prestige. He was aware of the condition of people who looked like him; from Bani Isra'il, who were in slavery and killed. He knew he was privileged but he did not forget his place. This is a very important lesson. Sometimes, when you make it 'big', you tend to forget where you came from. This makes you ungrateful. Then, you would claim, "I did this. I achieved this. All by myself." You start to attribute things to yourself. Remember that this is all Allah. It is Him who blessed you with all things favours.

If you come from the downtrodden and you become from the privileged, then you disown the downtrodden, it is like you hate yourself. You hate your own identity. You hate these people, thinking, "Why didn't they just earn and do this the way I did? Why didn't they pick themselves up?" So Musa (a.s.) was saying that he was never going to become one of the tyrants or side with them as a result of this.

My Lord is with Me

$$\text{فَأَصْبَحَ فِى ٱلْمَدِينَةِ خَائِفًا يَتَرَقَّبُ فَإِذَا ٱلَّذِى ٱسْتَنصَرَهُۥ بِٱلْأَمْسِ يَسْتَصْرِخُهُۥ ۚ قَالَ لَهُۥ مُوسَىٰٓ إِنَّكَ لَغَوِىٌّ مُّبِينٌ ﴿١٨﴾}$$

And he became inside the city fearful and anticipating [exposure], when suddenly the one who sought his help the previous day cried out to him [once again]. Moses said to him, "Indeed, you are an evident, [persistent] deviator."

(al-Qaṣaṣ, 28:17)

Allah (s.w.t.) then went on with the story that is recorded in *surah* al-Qaṣaṣ. Musa (a.s.) became fearful; watching out over his shoulder. He was constantly watching over his back. He was alone, walking in the streets. So far, no one knows about the murder except for the man he helped. So he was hoping that the man he saved would keep the murder quiet. It was for his sake anyway. Suddenly, he saw the man he saved again, being attacked by another Egyptian man. He saw Musa (a.s.), and was calling out to him for help.

What would you do if you were in Musa's (a.s.) place?

So Musa (a.s.) looked at the situation and said, "You are a troublemaker," to the man from Bani Isra'il, then charged at both of them. Looking at that, the man from Bani Isra'il shouted, "Are you going to kill me like you killed the man from yesterday?"

فَلَمَّآ أَنْ أَرَادَ أَن يَبْطِشَ بِٱلَّذِى هُوَ عَدُوٌّ لَّهُمَا قَالَ يَٰمُوسَىٰٓ أَتُرِيدُ أَن تَقْتُلَنِى كَمَا قَتَلْتَ نَفْسًۢا بِٱلْأَمْسِ ۖ إِن تُرِيدُ إِلَّآ أَن تَكُونَ جَبَّارًا فِى ٱلْأَرْضِ وَمَا تُرِيدُ أَن تَكُونَ مِنَ ٱلْمُصْلِحِينَ ۝

> And when he wanted to strike the one who was an enemy to both of them, he said, "O' Moses, do you intend to kill me as you killed someone yesterday? You only want to be a tyrant in the land and do not want to be of the amenders."
>
> (al-Qaṣaṣ, 28:19)

Musa (a.s.) was actually trying to save him from the Egyptian man. However, the man from Bani Isra'il misunderstood the situation. He saw Musa (a.s.) charging at them both, and remembered how Musa (a.s.) killed the attacker yesterday with a punch so he wanted to slow him down. Unfortunately, this man has caused Musa (a.s.) into more trouble. The Egyptian man in front of them heard this and immediately went running back towards the authorities, to inform them that Musa (a.s.) was the one who killed the Egyptian man yesterday.

Now, put yourself in Musa's (a.s.) shoes. What are you going to do? Do you run for your life or do you kill the man from Bani Isra'il?

Sometimes, we get so obsessed with someone who caused us tragedy. But we did not reflect on the

lessons that we could learn from it. Take the Prophet's (s.a.w.) situation. He (s.a.w.) could have harboured many bitter feelings towards people of Taif. Instead, he made *du'a'* for them. He (s.a.w.) looked forward to the day of them guiding him. Even though they spat and hit him, he focused on the lesson Allah was trying to teach him at that moment. He (s.a.w.) reflected, "How do I observe patience in this situation?"

Important note: This does not mean accepting zulm or wrongdoings to befallen onto you.

We sometimes even say things like, "If this person did not show up, my life would have been so much better. I would have never had hardship. Life would have been amazing." While maybe that person does deserve a lot of blame, and carry the burden of their sin, but for your own *tazkiyah*, focus more on getting closer to Allah (s.w.t.) through the situation. Saying 'if' also opens the door of *shaytan* as mentioned in the Prophet's (s.a.w.) hadith:

> It was narrated that Abu Hurayrah (r.a.) said:
>
> "The Messenger of Allah (s.a.w.) said: 'The strong believer is better and more beloved to Allah than the weak believer, although both

are good. Strive for that which will benefit you, seek the help of Allah, and do not feel helpless. If anything befalls you, do not say, 'If only I had done such and such' rather say '*Qaddara Allāhu wa mā shā fa'ala* (Allah has decreed and whatever he wills, He does).' For (saying) 'If' opens (the door) to the deeds of *shayṭan*."

(Sunan Ibn Majah 79)

So Musa (a.s.) was still focused on Allah (s.w.t.) when the Egyptian man went to signal the authorities.

وَجَآءَ رَجُلٌ مِّنْ أَقْصَا ٱلْمَدِينَةِ يَسْعَىٰ قَالَ يَٰمُوسَىٰٓ إِنَّ ٱلْمَلَأَ يَأْتَمِرُونَ بِكَ لِيَقْتُلُوكَ فَٱخْرُجْ إِنِّى لَكَ مِنَ ٱلنَّـٰصِحِينَ ۝

And a man came from the farthest end of the city, running. He said, "O' Moses, indeed the eminent ones are conferring over you [intending] to kill you, so leave [the city]; indeed, I am to you of the sincere advisors."

(al-Qaṣaṣ, 28:20)

Another man heard the decree and advised Musa (a.s.) to flee. However, Musa (a.s.) was flummoxed. "What do you mean, leave? Where should I go?"

Musa (a.s.) had no one in this world. He could not take a ship or take a flight somewhere. But the man was insisting that he would not win the battle—in case Musa (a.s.) was trying to make an argument or explain the situation.

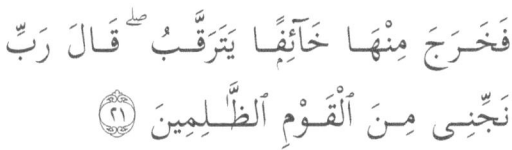

So he left it, fearful and anticipating [apprehension]. He said, "My Lord, save me from the wrongdoing people."

(al-Qaṣaṣ, 28:21)

Allah (s.w.t.) then said, Musa (a.s.) left the city feeling scared. Imagine the fear he went through—how he kept looking over his shoulders to see if anyone was behind him.

As humans, we are affected by fear to a great extent. We cannot sleep, we get paranoid, we are anxious. It was the same with Musa (a.s.). He knew the monstrosities Fir'awn committed to people. If they found him, they would execute him the same. So he said:

"My Lord, save me from the wrongdoing people."

In his journey of saving himself, Musa (a.s.) was directed towards Madyan. He did not know where he was actually going, but he marched on.

$$وَلَمَّا تَوَجَّهَ تِلْقَاءَ مَدْيَنَ قَالَ عَسَىٰ رَبِّىٓ أَن يَهْدِيَنِى سَوَآءَ ٱلسَّبِيلِ ۝$$

And when he directed himself toward Madyan, he said, "Perhaps my Lord will guide me to the sound way."

(al-Qaṣaṣ, 28:22)

From the verse, one can see that Musa (a.s.) was putting his utmost trust to his Lord to guide him to the right path.

$$\text{فَلَمَّا تَرَٰٓءَا ٱلْجَمْعَانِ قَالَ أَصْحَٰبُ مُوسَىٰٓ إِنَّا لَمُدْرَكُونَ ﴿٦١﴾}$$

And when the two companies saw one another, the companions of Moses said, "Indeed, we are to be overtaken!"

(ash-Shuʿara', 26:61)

The same thing happened later on where you can see Musa (a.s.) in front of the Red Sea. They were saying to Musa (a.s.), "We're done. They caught us." In this situation, Musa (a.s.) was looking over his shoulder to see the Egyptian troops. Sometimes, people's words are a *fitnah* for you.

"You are done. You have no hope. You are in trouble."

But do you know what Musa (a.s.) said?

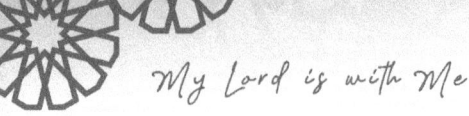

My Lord is with Me

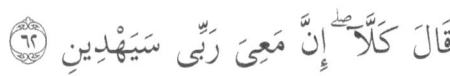

[Moses] said, "No! Indeed, with me is my Lord; He will guide me."

(ash-Shu'ara', 26:62)

Musa (a.s.) knew that Allah (s.w.t.) is with him and going to guide him. *Tawakkul* is the oxygen of your *du'a'*. You have to put your absolute trust in Allah (s.w.t.) because no matter how good your *du'a'* sound or which script you read, your *du'a'* is meaningless without your trust in Allah.

> *Tawakkul is the oxygen of your duʿāʾ.*

As Ibn Qayyim (r.a.h.) says:

If you were to trust Allah the way that He deserves to be trusted, Allah would move mountains for you.

'Umar ibn al-Khaṭṭab (r.a.) reported:

> The Messenger of Allah, peace and blessings be upon him, said, "If you were to rely upon Allah with reliance due to Him, He would provide for you just as He provides for the birds. They go out in the morning with empty stomachs and return full."

(Sunan al-Tirmidhi 2344)

Trust in Allah is the oxygen of your *du'a'*. Sometimes you find your *du'a'* does not 'work'. But the problem is not about the *du'a'* itself. It is about the distrust and doubt that you have while you are asking Allah. You lack an important ingredient which is *tawakkul*. Musa (a.s.) on the other hand had full trust in Allah (s.w.t.) as he was going into the situation. So Allah (s.w.t.) said that he made it to Madyan.

وَلَمَّا وَرَدَ مَاءَ مَدْيَنَ وَجَدَ عَلَيْهِ أُمَّةً مِّنَ ٱلنَّاسِ يَسْقُونَ وَوَجَدَ مِن دُونِهِمُ

DR. OMAR SULEIMAN

ٱمْرَأَتَيْنِ تَذُودَانِ ۖ قَالَ مَا خَطْبُكُمَا ۖ قَالَتَا لَا نَسْقِى حَتَّىٰ يُصْدِرَ ٱلرِّعَآءُ ۖ وَأَبُونَا شَيْخٌ كَبِيرٌ ﴿٢٣﴾

And when he came to the water [i.e., well] of Madyan, he found there a crowd of people watering [their flocks], and he found aside from them two women holding back [their flocks]. He said, "What is your circumstance?" They said, "We do not water until the shepherds dispatch [their flocks]; and our father is an old man."

(al-Qaṣaṣ, 28:23)

Madyan is the first city outside of the control of Firʿawn. At that moment, he had escaped the legion of Firʿawn, but that did not necessarily stop him. But it was better than being under Egyptian rule. So when he reached there, he saw a well, surrounded by a crowd trying to get water from it. There were two shy women waiting with their flocks. Musa (a.s.) asked them, "What's wrong?" So they told him that they were waiting for everyone to get through which would take hours. They were shy, and their father was an old man. So Musa (a.s.)—being a strong man he was—got through the crown and got the water for them.

Musa (a.s.) was a fugitive, running for his life at that moment. Other people would just think of themselves, but Musa (a.s.) still had the time to spare to help others.

Nowadays, people have a twisted view of doing good deeds. Quotes like "*the empath suffers*" and "*no good deed goes unpunished*" colour how people see life. Popular culture, on the other hand, promotes the concept of "*be yourself*" or "*do yourself.*" As long as it makes you happy, everything is permissible. You could ignore the world even if it burns down if that makes you happy. This is now the concept of *du'a'*, charity, and spirituality many of us adopt, which feeds into narcissism. This is something Musa (a.s.) was never interested in. He was always looking to serve, always looking to help which is a beautiful quality.

It can get you in trouble sometimes, like Musa (a.s.) with the Egyptian man and the Bani Isra'il man. Sometimes it can be really, really good for you. In all times it can be to your benefit if you turn towards Allah (s.w.t.) seeking His reward.

The Prophet (s.a.w.) said:

> Abu Dharr reported: The Messenger of Allah (s.a.w.) said, "Fear Allah wherever you are, follow a bad deed with a good deed and it will erase it, and behave with good character towards people."
>
> (Sunan al-Tirmidhi 1987)

So Musa (a.s.) is the best epitome regarding the hadith—he was observing *taqwa* wherever he was and in every situation and he followed a bad deed with a good deed. Musa (a.s.) killed a man and was a fugitive. Then he followed up his mistake with a good deed. This is because the mistake of turning away from Allah (s.w.t.) would have been greater. So don't you dare turn away from Allah (s.w.t.). Even the man who killed ninety-nine people—he was not trying to help anybody—turned back to Allah (s.w.t.) and it was the best decision he made for his afterlife.

As for Musa (a.s.), he did not ignore the situation. Helping the two women probably puts him at a greater risk. What if he gets into more trouble? He was not from them. What if they start fighting him? What if he gets reported that he was a fugitive of Fir'awn?

Musa (a.s.) could have practised apathy and turned away from the situation, but he did not.

In this world, we are all weaved together. Maybe you are the answer to someone's prayers. You have no idea what is your role in someone else's relationship with Allah (s.w.t.) but our lives often intersect. Possibly, Musa (a.s.) was the answer to the women's *du'a'*. So trust Allah (s.w.t.), He is the Designer.

After Musa (a.s.) helped the women with water, he right away went to the shade without waiting for payment or reward. He was probably hungry or thirsty; he might as well ask them for some tips. But he did not. He did everything for the sake of Allah (s.w.t.). At the corner, under the shade, Musa (a.s.) recited one of the most beautiful *du'a'* in the Qur'an:

$$\text{فَسَقَىٰ لَهُمَا ثُمَّ تَوَلَّىٰٓ إِلَى ٱلظِّلِّ فَقَالَ رَبِّ إِنِّى لِمَآ أَنزَلۡتَ إِلَىَّ مِنۡ خَيۡرٖ فَقِيرٞ ﴿٢٤﴾}$$

So he watered [their flocks] for them; then he went back to the shade and said, "My Lord, indeed I am, for whatever good You would send down to me, in need."

(al-Qaṣaṣ, 28:24)

Musa (a.s.) was saying, O' my Lord, I am for whatever good you are going to send me. I am completely in need of it—whatever you have in store for me. I am desperate for it.

Firstly, regarding this *du'a'*, who knew that it would be immortalised in the Qur'an? It was just Musa (a.s.), a fugitive, calling upon Allah under the shade. It is not a very profound *du'a'* in terms of meaning. But you can see the desperation in it, the way it is worded. "For whatever good". Musa (a.s.) did not know what good means anymore at that point and he had no idea how to get out of the situation, but, with his utmost trust in Allah (s.w.t.), he believed that whatever comes next from Allah is the best for him. This might mean being put in the river again, or something is going to rain upon him, or something he has no idea about. But he knew, he was desperately in need of it. Readers, this is one of the most important *du'a'* in our life.

Breaking it down, it describes Musa's (a.s.) situation. Musa (a.s.) expressed his brokenness. And when you are broken before Allah, He will not shatter you further but rather mends you. However, that sense of brokenness before Allah (s.w.t.) is crucial. Scholars note that Musa (a.s.) acknowledged his dependency

My Lord is with Me

in every circumstance—whether in the palace, by the river, in safety or danger, as a prophet or a fugitive. He constantly relied on Allah (s.w.t.), never claiming independence, and his need for Allah (s.w.t.) never diminished from one day to the next.

Reflect on this. Sometimes, we only feel the urgency of needing Allah (s.w.t.) during hardship. But when we are comfortable, our prayers may lack fervour.

اللَّهُمَّ إِنِّي أَسْلَمْتُ نَفْسِي إِلَيْكَ وَوَجَّهْتُ وَجْهِي إِلَيْكَ وَفَوَّضْتُ أَمْرِي إِلَيْكَ رَغْبَةً وَرَهْبَةً إِلَيْكَ وَأَلْجَأْتُ ظَهْرِي إِلَيْكَ لاَ مَلْجَأَ وَلاَ مَنْجَا مِنْكَ إِلاَّ إِلَيْكَ آمَنْتُ بِكِتَابِكَ الَّذِي أَنْزَلْتَ وَبِنَبِيِّكَ الَّذِي أَرْسَلْتَ

'O Allah, verily, I submit myself to You, and I turn my face to You, and I entrust my affair to You, hoping in You and fearing in You. And I lay myself down depending upon You, there is no refuge [nor escape] from You except to

You. I believe in Your Book which You have revealed, and in Your Prophet whom You have sent.'

(Jami' at-Tirmidhi 3394)

Now, Musa (a.s.) was caught in a rut due to his mistake. Yet, observe his *du'a'*. He turned to Allah, simply asking for whatever goodness Allah will send his way, when he, as a prophet of Allah, can be specific with his request.

Sometimes we are too specific with our prayers as if we know what's best for us. I recall my experience with a brother inquiring about performing *Salat al-Istikharah*. So I shared the supplication: "O' Allah, if it's good for me, make it easy, and if it's not, remove it from me." But the brother pleaded, "*Shaykh*, I only want her. Please don't take her away." What's the point of *istikharah* when you have a lack of trust in Allah?

While specificity is not wrong—consider the story of a *ṣaḥabah* who requested Allah to mend his shoelace. This means that he was comfortable seeking Allah's help for all his needs, knowing that nothing is too much for Him. However, it becomes problematic when we put conditions on Allah in granting our prayers.

Remember Sulayman (a.s.) who simply asked for a good kingdom from Allah. Had he been overly specific, the outcome might have been limited. Instead, Allah granted him an unprecedented kingdom. Sometimes, the best prayers are the general ones. It is narrated in a hadith (Ṣaḥīḥ al-Bukhari 6389) that the most frequent supplication of the Prophet (s.a.w.) was:

رَبَّنَا آتِنَا فِي الدُّنْيَا حَسَنَةً، وَفِي الآخِرَةِ حَسَنَةً، وَقِنَا عَذَابَ النَّارِ ﴿٢٠١﴾

"O' Allah! Grant us goodness in this world and goodness in the Hereafter, and save us from the torment of the Fire."

(al-Baqarah, 2:201)

Shaykh Yasir Birjas once shared a man's prayer that goes something along this line:

"O' Allah, You already know and I already know. So there's no need for me to go further."

This is a good epitome of taking generality too far. So ask Allah (s.w.t.) for the best in this life and the next, and put your utmost trust on Him.

As Musa (a.s.) asked Allah (s.w.t.) for whatever good Allah will send him, that could mean anything—Fir'awn pardoning him, someone giving him money or direction for him to escape safely, or maybe just some group accepting him as a clan. But do you know what the *khayr* Allah sent him?

A wife!

Musa (a.s.) was not even requesting a wife. In his circumstances, a wife may not have crossed his mind. Look at the next *ayah* of *surah* al-Qaṣaṣ comes:

فَجَاءَتْهُ إِحْدَاهُمَا تَمْشِى عَلَى ٱسْتِحْيَاءٍ قَالَتْ إِنَّ أَبِى يَدْعُوكَ لِيَجْزِيَكَ أَجْرَ مَا سَقَيْتَ لَنَا ۚ فَلَمَّا جَاءَهُ وَقَصَّ عَلَيْهِ ٱلْقَصَصَ قَالَ لَا تَخَفْ ۖ نَجَوْتَ مِنَ ٱلْقَوْمِ ٱلظَّالِمِينَ ۝

> Then one of the two women came to him walking with shyness. She said, "Indeed, my father invites you that he may reward you for having watered for us." So when he came to him and related to him the story, he said, "Fear not. You have escaped from the wrongdoing people."

So one of the two women came quickly to him, telling him that their father was calling Musa (a.s.) and wanted to compensate him. Musa (a.s.) ended up telling everything that had happened to the old man, and the old man told Musa (a.s.): "Don't worry, you are now safe from the oppressing people."

How impressive it is, that this stranger is telling Musa (a.s.) the answer to his prayer? Musa (a.s.) previously asked that he be saved from the oppressing people. After his *du'a'*, Allah (s.w.t.) granted Musa (a.s.) with the answer that He sees fit.

So, to those in search for a good *du'a'* for marriage, I repeat it for you:

$$رَبِّ إِنِّى لِمَآ أَنزَلْتَ إِلَىَّ مِنْ خَيْرٍ فَقِيرٌ$$

> My Lord, indeed I am, for whatever good You would send down to me, in need.

So, Musa (a.s.) was in Madyan, where he got married and served his father-in-law. His life story, filled with significant events, becomes even more interesting as he goes through various stages.

This will be a summary of the historical events that happened as well as the nature of *du'a'*. This story of Musa (a.s.) is recorded in *surah* Ṭaha, 20:9-36.

While Musa (a.s.) was leaving Madyan, walking with his new family, he saw a fire or a burning bush. So he (a.s.) said:

$$\text{إِنِّىٓ ءَانَسْتُ نَارًا...}$$

"Indeed, I have perceived a fire."

$$\text{لَّعَلِّىٓ ءَاتِيكُم مِّنْهَا بِقَبَسٍ أَوْ أَجِدُ عَلَى النَّارِ هُدًى ﴿١٠﴾}$$

"Perhaps I can bring you a torch or find at the fire some guidance."

(Ṭaha, 20:10)

SubḥānAllāh, he understood that Allah was putting things in his path. When Musa (a.s.) arrived, Allah (s.w.t.) addressed him directly. Musa (a.s.) was in a situation where he was in conversation with his Lord directly and asked to see Him. Musa's (a.s.) request was out of a longing to increase in closeness and faith, not out of challenge or insecurity.

Allah (s.w.t.) told Musa (a.s.) to look at the mountain. If it stayed in its place, he would see Him. When Allah (s.w.t.) manifested a small part of His glory to the mountain, it crumbled, and Musa (a.s.) collapsed unconscious. When he awoke, he said:

$$...سُبْحَٰنَكَ تُبْتُ إِلَيْكَ وَأَنَا۠ أَوَّلُ ٱلْمُؤْمِنِينَ ۝${143}$$

"Exalted are You! I have repented to You, and I am the first of the believers."

(al-A'raf, 7:143)

This shows that Musa (a.s.) was not questioning Allah (s.w.t.) but sought *tawbah* if there was anything inappropriate in his request. At the fire, Musa (a.s.) heard a voice:

"O' Musa."

(Ṭaha, 20:11)

Musa (a.s.) was shocked by this direct conversation from Allah (s.w.t.). Allah said:

$$\text{إِنِّىٓ أَنَا۠ رَبُّكَ فَٱخْلَعْ نَعْلَيْكَ ۖ إِنَّكَ بِٱلْوَادِ ٱلْمُقَدَّسِ طُوًى ﴿١٢﴾}$$

"Indeed, I am your Lord, so remove your sandals. Indeed, you are in the sacred valley of Ṭuwa."

(Ṭaha, 20:12)

$$\text{وَأَنَا ٱخْتَرْتُكَ فَٱسْتَمِعْ لِمَا يُوحَىٰٓ ﴿١٣﴾}$$

"And I have chosen you, so listen to what is revealed [to you]."

(Ṭaha, 20:13)

$$\text{إِنَّنِىٓ أَنَا ٱللَّهُ لَآ إِلَٰهَ إِلَّآ أَنَا۠ فَٱعْبُدْنِى وَأَقِمِ ٱلصَّلَوٰةَ لِذِكْرِىٓ ﴿١٤﴾}$$

"Indeed, I am Allah. There is no deity except Me, so worship Me and establish prayer for My remembrance."

(Ṭaha, 20:14)

SubḥānAllāh. Musa (a.s.) heard this directly from Allah. Then Allah continued:

$$\text{إِنَّ ٱلسَّاعَةَ ءَاتِيَةٌ أَكَادُ أُخْفِيهَا لِتُجْزَىٰ كُلُّ نَفْسٍۭ بِمَا تَسْعَىٰ ﴿١٥﴾}$$

"Indeed, the Hour is coming—I almost conceal it—so that every soul may be recompensed according to that for which it strives."

(Ṭaha, 20:15)

$$\text{فَلَا يَصُدَّنَّكَ عَنْهَا مَن لَّا يُؤْمِنُ بِهَا وَٱتَّبَعَ هَوَىٰهُ فَتَرْدَىٰ ﴿١٦﴾}$$

"So do not let one avert you from it who does not believe in it and follows his desire, for you [then] would perish."

(Ṭaha, 20:16)

After this reminder, Allah gave Musa a miracle:

$$\text{وَمَا تِلْكَ بِيَمِينِكَ يَٰمُوسَىٰ} \; (17)$$

"And what is that in your right hand, O' Musa?"

(Ṭaha, 20:17)

Musa (a.s.) could have simply said, "It's a stick." But he wanted to prolong the conversation with Allah (s.w.t.), enjoying the Divine communication. He described his staff in detail, expressing his delight in speaking to Allah (s.w.t.).

Then Allah said, "Throw it down, O' Musa." When Musa (a.s.) did so, it became a snake that moved swiftly. Musa (a.s.) ran away, but Allah (s.w.t.) told him:

$$\text{قَالَ خُذْهَا وَلَا تَخَفْ سَنُعِيدُهَا سِيرَتَهَا ٱلْأُولَىٰ} \; (21)$$

"Seize it and fear not; We will return it to its former condition."

(Ṭaha, 20:21)

Allah was training Musa (a.s.). This encounter was a precursor to facing Fir'awn. Musa (a.s.)

needed to overcome any fear through his trust in Allah's command.

Allah then said:

$$\text{وَٱضْمُمْ يَدَكَ إِلَىٰ جَنَاحِكَ تَخْرُجْ بَيْضَاۤءَ مِنْ غَيْرِ سُوۤءٍ...}$$

"And draw in your hand to your side; it will come out white without disease..."

(Ṭaha, 20:22)

These miracles were shown to Musa (a.s.) to strengthen his faith and prepare him for his mission. Allah then commanded:

$$\text{ٱذْهَبْ إِلَىٰ فِرْعَوْنَ إِنَّهُۥ طَغَىٰ ﴿٢٤﴾}$$

"Go to Firʿawn. Indeed, he has transgressed."

(Ṭaha, 20:24)

Musa (a.s.) was to speak to Firʿawn, who had greatly transgressed. Despite Firʿawn's tyranny, Allah instructed Musa (a.s.) to speak gently to him:

$$\text{فَقُولَا لَهُۥ قَوْلًا لَّيِّنًا لَّعَلَّهُۥ يَتَذَكَّرُ أَوْ يَخْشَىٰ ﴿٤٤﴾}$$

"And speak to him with gentle speech that perhaps he may be reminded or fear [Allah]."

(Ṭaha, 20:44)

This teaches us the importance of *naṣiḥah* and the manner in which it should be given. When offering advice, it should come from a place of care and compassion, aiming to guide and uplift rather than condemn.

Musa (a.s.) made a beautiful *du'a'* that is often recited before undertaking difficult tasks:

$$\text{رَبِّ ٱشْرَحْ لِى صَدْرِى ﴿٢٥﴾ وَيَسِّرْ لِىٓ أَمْرِى ﴿٢٦﴾ وَٱحْلُلْ عُقْدَةً مِّن لِّسَانِى ﴿٢٧﴾ يَفْقَهُوا۟ قَوْلِى ﴿٢٨﴾}$$

"My Lord, expand for me my chest [with assurance] and ease for me my task and untie the knot from my tongue that they may understand my speech."

(Ṭaha, 20:25-28)

This *du'a'* emphasises the importance of inner faith and sincerity. Before addressing external challenges, one's heart must be open and filled with faith. Effective *da'wah* requires a heartfelt connection and genuine concern for others.

Musa (a.s.) then requested:

وَاجْعَل لِّى وَزِيرًا مِّنْ أَهْلِى ۝ هَٰرُونَ أَخِى ۝ اشْدُدْ بِهِ أَزْرِى ۝ وَأَشْرِكْهُ فِىٓ أَمْرِى ۝ كَىْ نُسَبِّحَكَ كَثِيرًا ۝ وَنَذْكُرَكَ كَثِيرًا ۝ إِنَّكَ كُنتَ بِنَا بَصِيرًا ۝

"And appoint for me a minister from my family—Harun, my brother. Increase through him my strength and let him share my task that we may exalt You much and remember You much. Indeed, You are of us ever Seeing."

(Taha, 20:29-35)

Musa (a.s.) asked for support from his brother Harun (a.s.), demonstrating the importance of having righteous companions. This request was not to shirk from his responsibility, in this case, talking to Firʿawn but to enhance the mission with the support of a trusted and pious companion.

One of the *salaf* said, "There is no one who has ever done a greater favour to his brother than Musa did for Harun, may peace be upon them both, for he interceded for him until Allah made him a Prophet and Messenger with him to Firʿawn and his chiefs."

Finally, we come to the last two situations:

1. Musa (a.s.) and the Red Sea

Allah (s.w.t.) saved Musa (a.s.) through the Red Sea:

> *My Lord is with me, and He will guide me.*

Allah (s.w.t.) guided Musa (a.s.) and his people away from Firʿawn and his army, and He drowned them. From this story, one profound lesson we must reflect on is that as believers, we often focus so much on the enemy that we neglect the spiritual ills within our own communities. We make it seem like if the *kuffar* left us alone, we would be successful in achieving anything we could dream of. However, in reality, we have often adopted, ingested, and applied the same evils employed against us collectively as an *ummah*. We mistreat each other in the exact same ways we are mistreated on the outside. So, you can't always blame your enemy. There is no Firʿawn and his army to blame anymore.

In the story of Musa (a.s.), it was just him and Bani Isra'il. Allah showed them a great miracle through their prophet. And what did they do? They started giving Musa (a.s.) a hard time. Some unrectified spiritual ills began to emerge among them—the corruption, the arrogance, the greed. They had learned the ways of their oppressors. Sometimes people complain about corrupt leadership without realising they might be just as corrupt if they were in the same position. Consider political corruption, for instance. But are you just as corrupt? Would you do the exact same things if you had access to power? Look at the way Muslims mistreat each other—the gossip, the mistreatment, the oppression. What makes us different from the way Islamophobes and enemies of Islam treat us? We talk so much about the outside, but we don't rectify the inside.

$$إِنَّ ٱللَّهَ لَا يُغَيِّرُ مَا بِقَوْمٍ حَتَّىٰ يُغَيِّرُوا۟ مَا بِأَنفُسِهِمْ ۗ ...$$

"Indeed, Allah will not change the condition of a people until they change what is in themselves."

(ar-Ra'd, 13:11)

Allah does not change the condition of a people until they change what is within themselves. This does not mean letting oppression happen or ignoring the enemy; it means stay focused on the greater enemy within. This has to be your priority because if you overcome that, then what harms you is merely a blessing and elevation, not a consequence of your evil. So, focus on that individually.

So here they are, Bani Isra'il with Musa (a.s.).

Think about this: they just watched a man with a staff touch the sea; the Red Sea split in half, they walked through it, and it drowned the most powerful tyrant in the world. And then Musa (a.s.) goes to his Lord.

Bani Israil immediately say, "Let's build a golden calf. Let's build an idol."

They had become so accustomed—their mentality—to the ways of those they deemed superior that they were willing to risk the anger of Allah to do that. Musa (a.s.) thought, "What's the worst these people can do if I leave them for a month?" He came back to find them worshipping a golden calf. Obviously, he turned his anger to Harun (a.s.) because he had left him in charge. In his grief, Musa (a.s.)

broke the tablets from his Lord and grabbed Harun (a.s.) by the hair, dragging him in anger. "How could you let this happen? I leave you people for one month, and you return to the shirk of your oppressors who are not even your forefathers. This isn't even the shirk of your fathers. This is the shirk of the people who enslaved you, and you go back to that?"

That is the mentality of an oppressed people with colonised mindsets and slave mentality. They adopt the ways of those they deem their superiors instead of seeing Allah as greater than all of them. Harun (a.s.) pleaded for Musa (a.s.) to stop because he was saying: "It's not just that they overcame me and I was unable to stop them, but it's more important that we don't let this display of us fighting be to the joy of these oppressive people. They love to see us fight." You know what your enemies love? They love to see internal disputes because now we do their job for them. The Prophet (s.a.w.) once asked Allah for three things:

He (s.a.w.) asked Allah (s.w.t.):

1. To protect his *ummah* from an enemy that would wipe them off the face of the Earth.

    And Allah granted him that.

2. To protect them from famine or plague that would wipe them all off the face of the Earth.

    And Allah granted him that.

3. To not let their misfortune be among themselves.

    But Allah did not grant the Prophet (s.a.w.) that.

Why, you may ask?

Because you have to clean up your own mess as a community. So here Harun (a.s.) was saying to Musa (a.s.), "Don't let them find joy in watching us fight. I'm not your enemy, O' Musa. I'm your brother and a prophet of Allah. The enemy is the one who invited them to the *shirk*. The enemy is the *shirk* itself. The enemy is the factor that led to this. Let's deal with that."

Musa (a.s.) then made the following supplication:

قَالَ رَبِّ ٱغْفِرْ لِى وَلِأَخِى وَأَدْخِلْنَا فِى رَحْمَتِكَ ۖ وَأَنتَ أَرْحَمُ ٱلرَّٰحِمِينَ ﴿١٥١﴾

> [Moses] said, "My Lord, forgive me and my brother and admit us into Your mercy, for You are the most merciful of the merciful."
>
> (al-A'raf, 7:151)

What does it mean to "admit us into Your mercy"?

Allah (s.w.t.) refers to *Jannah* as His mercy. In an authentic hadith, Allah (s.w.t.) said to *Jannah*, "You are My mercy, I enter into you whomever I please." This is why we pray that Allah admits us into His mercy, for He is the Most Merciful of those who show mercy.

Musa (a.s.) had to remember that this task does not guarantee a worldly outcome, but it certainly has an outcome in the hereafter. The hereafter's outcome for a person is patience, and a person strives in a way that is pleasing to Allah (s.w.t.).

This marks the last part of Musa's (a.s.) supplication.

According to the Qur'an, Bani Isra'il were condemned to wander in the desert for 40 years as a consequence of their disobedience and lack of faith. This event is primarily detailed in *surah* al-Ma'idah, verses 20-26.

Allah (s.w.t.) said that Musa (a.s.) said to his people, "O' my people, enter the Holy Land that Allah has written for you."

Allah has prepared the land for them, so they don't have to worry about anything else. However, they responded, "But there are mighty people there, and we will not enter until they leave. If they leave, then we will enter."

SubḥānAllāh. Allah had shown them what He did to Firʿawn and his army, but they did not heed the lessons.

How many people do you think were with Musa (a.s.) at this point? According to Ibn Abbas (r.a.), up to 600,000 people were unwilling to enter with Musa (a.s.). He looked around at a whole *ummah*, and they did not want to go with him into the land that had been written for them. Only two people came forward that were willing to enter alongside him. They said to Musa (a.s.), "Go ahead, you and your Lord, and fight. We'll wait for you over here." Imagine how much that hurt?

Do you know the story of Miqdad?

It was during the Battle of Badr, which was one of the earliest and most significant battles in Islamic history. Before the battle commenced, the

Prophet (s.a.w.) consulted his companions about their readiness to confront the Quraysh. Miqdad's response was particularly notable.

Miqdad said, "O' Messenger of Allah, we will not say to you what the people of Musa said to Musa: 'Go, you and your Lord, and fight. Indeed, we are sitting right here.' But we will say: 'Go, you and your Lord, and fight, and we will fight along with you.' By Allah, if you were to lead us to Birk al-Ghimad (a place far in Yemen), we would follow you."

This hadith is recorded in Ṣaḥiḥ al-Bukhari 3952.

Looking at the situation, Musa (a.s.) looked up to Allah (s.w.t.) and said, "O' my Lord, I do not control anyone but myself and my brother. I have no control over these people. It's me and my brother, so distinguish between us and the evildoers." Musa (a.s.) pleaded to not be not considered among these people.

It is such a powerful statement.

Zaynab (r.a.) once asked the Prophet (s.a.w.), "Will we be destroyed when we have righteous people among us?" The Prophet (s.a.w.) said, "Yes, if filth becomes prevalent."

This is mentioned in Ṣaḥiḥ al-Bukhari 7135.

When large groups of people die, the righteous among them will be raised according to their righteousness. So Musa was concerned that he and his brother Harun (a.s.) would be resurrected with these people. They might suffer the worldly consequence of being with Bani Isra'il for the next forty years in this exodus. But at the same time, they did not want to be considered among them.

Allah (s.w.t.) answered with what is known as *sunnatul-istibdal*, meaning the law of Allah in changing worthy people.

يَٰٓأَيُّهَا ٱلَّذِينَ ءَامَنُواْ مَن يَرْتَدَّ مِنكُمْ عَن دِينِهِۦ فَسَوْفَ يَأْتِى ٱللَّهُ بِقَوْمٍ يُحِبُّهُمْ وَيُحِبُّونَهُۥٓ أَذِلَّةٍ عَلَى ٱلْمُؤْمِنِينَ أَعِزَّةٍ عَلَى ٱلْكَٰفِرِينَ يُجَٰهِدُونَ فِى سَبِيلِ ٱللَّهِ وَلَا يَخَافُونَ لَوْمَةَ لَآئِمٍ ۚ ذَٰلِكَ فَضْلُ ٱللَّهِ يُؤْتِيهِ مَن يَشَآءُ ۚ وَٱللَّهُ وَٰسِعٌ عَلِيمٌ ﴿٥٤﴾

O' you who have believed, whoever of you should revert from his religion—Allah will bring

> forth [in place of them] a people He will love and who will love Him [who are] humble toward the believers, strong against the disbelievers; they strive in the cause of Allah and do not fear the blame of a critic. That is the favour of Allah; He bestows it upon whom He wills. And Allah is all-Encompassing and Knowing.
>
> (al-Ma'idah: 5:54)

This means that if you are not up for the task, Allah will find people worthy of the task, and the work will still go forward. This is the thing about *da'wah* and good work. You will never harm Allah or make Him deficient with your disobedience. His dominion is untouched. So, you are never going to harm Allah when you turn away from good work and say, "I'll show them they won't be able to continue without me." No, Allah will find different people, and they will be better than you. Thus, Allah held Bani Isra'il back until another generation arose that had enough righteous people worthy of the task to go forward. So, in this situation, the people of Musa (a.s.) were all adults. They spent forty years in the desert, and this group of people perished. Another group of people emerged that were worthy of the task.

Last but not least, as a Palestinian who has never been able to enter Palestine, this is a very personal matter for me. May Allah grant us all entry into Al-Aqsa and liberate it. *Āmīn*.

Musa (a.s.) was in this desert, forbidden from Al-Quds because of his people. When death approached Musa (a.s.), his final supplication was to be as close to the Holy Land as possible. He prayed:

> "Let me be within a stone's throw of the Holy Land."

It is profoundly painful, *subḥānAllāh*. Musa (a.s.) was saying that is all he desired at that point.

> "I may not enter it, but O' Allah, let me die as close to it as possible."

The Prophet (a.s.) said, "I passed by the grave of Musa (a.s.) and it was at the red dune." (Sunan an-Nasa'i 1631) Biblical sources refer to this place as Mount Nebo. Musa (a.s.) passed away right on the outskirts of Jerusalem, just outside Al-Quds.

The fact that he desired to die so close to Al-Aqsa is very special. It was narrated in Ṣaḥīḥ Bukhari that Musa (a.s.) visited Makkah and performed *'umrah* or *ḥajj*, and while he visited the Ka'bah, his heart was attached to Al-Aqsa. It is a significant matter.

When people debate whether Palestine is a political or religious issue, it is indeed a religious issue. If Al-Aqsa means nothing to you, there is an issue with your heart. It is a sign of a deficiency in faith if Al-Aqsa means nothing to the believer's heart. It is not just another place; it is a sacred place that is occupied, where the blood of our brothers and sisters is unjustly spilled. You must be attached to it. If you are not, ask Allah to attach your heart to it and ask Allah to free and liberate it. But your heart must be attached to that place.

In his final supplication, Musa (a.s.) asked Allah, "O' Allah, let me die close to it. Let me die as close to it as possible."

My Lord is with Me

The beauty of Allah (s.w.t.), Who controls time and place, is that He let the Prophet Muhammad (s.a.w.) lead the prophets in *ṣalah* in Al-Aqsa. Musa (a.s.) was standing in the rows of prayer on the night of Isra' and Mi'raj. Imagine the Prophet Muhammad (s.a.w.) saying *Allāhu Akbar*, and the rows behind him included 'Isa (a.s.), Ibrahim (a.s.), and Musa (a.s.). What a momentous occasion. Unbelievable. *SubḥānAllāh*. Truly beautiful.

Dear brothers and sisters, this is, of course, a lesson for us regarding supplication and its outcomes. Allah did not grant Musa (a.s.) every outcome in this life, but He fulfilled everything He promised him and more, in terms of reward and elevation. May Allah grant us the same *yaqin* in our supplications as Musa (a.s.), as well as the same *tawakkul* in Allah. We ask Allah to grant us entry into the highest level of *Jannah* and to make our brother, Shaykh Muhammad AlShareef, among the righteous, reuniting our souls with the prophets, the righteous, and the martyrs. We ask Allah to liberate the land of the prophets, Al-Masjid Al-Aqsa, and to grant us the opportunity to pray in it, free from occupation and oppression. *Āmīn*.

Glossary

1. *Ayah:* Verse (Plural: *Ayat*)
2. *Barakah:* Blessings
3. *Daʿwah:* A call to embrace Islam
4. *Dhikr:* Remembrance to Allah
5. *Dīn:* Religion
6. *Duʿaʾ:* Supplication
7. *Fiqh:* Jurisprudence
8. *Fitnah:* Disgrace, humiliation
9. *Fitrah:* The innate human nature that recognises the oneness of Allah (s.w.t.)
10. *Ḥajj:* Pilgrimage to Makkah
11. *Imam:* One who leads Muslim worshippers in prayer. In a global sense, *imam* is used to refer to the head of the Muslim community (*ummah*)
12. *Khayr:* Goodness
13. *Kuffar:* Non-believers

14. *Ma'sum:* Infallible
15. *Naṣiḥah:* Sincere advice
16. *Qabilah:* Social organisation
17. *Qadar:* Divine decree
18. *Qiyamul-layl:* The period you dedicate praying to and remembering Allah between the completion of the *'Isha' ṣalah* and the break of dawn (*Fajr*)
19. *Ṣadaqah jariyah:* Ever-flowing charity
20. *Ṣaḥabah:* Companions
21. *Salaf:* Righteous predecessors
22. *Ṣalah:* Prayer
23. *Ṣalat al-Fajr:* Daily Islamic prayer offered in the early morning
24. *Ṣalat al-Istikharah:* Prayer of seeking counsel from Allah (s.w.t.)
25. *Shaykh:* A leader in a Muslim community or organisation
26. *Shayṭan:* The Devil
27. *Shirk:* Idolatry or polytheism
28. *Sunnatul-istibdal:* Allah's law of replacement

29. *Surah:* Chapters in the Qur'an
30. *Taqwa:* Forbearance, fear and abstinence from what Allah forbids
31. *Tawakkul:* Total reliance in Allah
32. *Tawbah:* Repentance
33. *Tazkiyah:* Purification
34. *Ummah:* Community
35. *Yaqin:* Certainty
36. *'Aqidah:* Islamic creed
37. *'Umrah:* A non-compulsory visit to Makkah unlike *Ḥajj*

www.ingramcontent.com/pod-product-compliance
Lightning Source LLC
LaVergne TN
LVHW061344080526
838199LV00094B/7350